WAITING FOR WAITING FOR GODOT

T0266567

Dave Hanson

WAITING FOR WAITING FOR GODOT

OBERON BOOKS
LONDON

WWW.OBERONBOOKS.COM

First published in 2016 by Oberon Books Ltd

521 Caledonian Road, London N7 9RH

Tel: +44 (0) 20 7607 3637 / Fax: +44 (0) 20 7607 3629

e-mail: info@oberonbooks.com

www.oberonbooks.com

PB ISBN: 9781786820419

E ISBN: 9781786820426

Cover design by Rebecca Pitt

eBook conversion by CPI Group (UK) Ltd, Croydon, CR0 4YY

This play is dedicated to my wife, Hillary.
I love you.

Waiting for Waiting for Godot
by Dave Hanson
Produced by Libby Brodie Productions.
Presented at the St. James Theatre, London, UK on 30
August 2016

Cast
Ester……..Simon Day
Val………….James Marlowe
Laura……..Laura Kirman

Directed by Mark Bell
Set & Costume Design by Sophia Simensky
Lighting Design by Charlie Hodsdon
Sound Design by Andrew Josephs

Waiting For Waiting For Godot was originally presented at
the 2013 New York International Fringe Festival.
A production of The Present Company.
Produced by Victoria Dicce and Hillary Burgess.

Cast
Ester…….Chris Sullivan
Val………….Dave Hanson
Laura……..Amy Weaver

Directed by Alex Harvey
Set & Costume Design by Tilly Grimes
Lighting Design by Dante Olivia Smith

Characters

ESTER

An Understudy

VAL

An Understudy

LAURA

The Assistant Stage Manager

Production Notes

Pg. 19 calls for characters to sing and hum the tune of "*There's No Business Like Show Business*". This can be accomplished by actually singing a few bars of the song or by lip-syncing a few bars of a recorded version of the song is up to the production's discretion.

The *Bust of Beethoven* should be of a size and weight that is easy for ESTER to carry and hold on to, but also be seen by the audience.

For the London production, certain words and references in the script were changed from American English phrases to equivalent U.K. English phrases. For reference please refer to the glossary at the back the script.

We are back stage of a local production of WAITING FOR GODOT. UP CENTER LEFT is a costume rack with an assortment of coats, costumes, shirts on it. CENTER RIGHT is a small chair and table with a script on it. Somewhere else is a metal stool to sit on. Around the room is an assortment of junk from previous productions (more costumes, props, boxes, trunks, random furniture, etc.). Several assorted lamps are turned on and light the space. Somewhere in the room is placed a small bust of Beethoven. From a back stage speaker, a performance of a play is heard in monotone. UPSTAGE, A door leads to a bathroom. A second entrance (either from STAGE LEFT or RIGHT or from the audience) leads to the rest of the theatre.

ACT ONE

In the darkness we hear a man struggling.

LIGHTS UP on ESTER, a large man, standing CENTER. He wears a bowler hat, long-underwear, and old, leather, shoes. He is wearing a vest that is too small. He struggles to button it, almost gets it, fails. He tries again, almost gets it, and fails. At some point, he hangs the vest up, walks away and tries a few actor warm-up exercises in a pretentious, over-pronouncing, voice, "Red Leather, Yellow Leather…", "The Big Black Bear…", sings a few voice warm-up scales, etc.

He looks at the vest. He puts the vest back on, tries again, fails. He takes the vest off to check that it is the right one. He begins again and fails. He takes the vest off, perplexed, gives it a good shake, tries again and fails. This continues.

VAL enters, dressed similar to ESTER, but wearing an old pair of pants, a bowler hat, but no vest. He carries two "to-go" coffee cups and a paper bag full of sugar packets and creams. VAL is more slender to ESTER's largeness and has a gentle naiveté about his face. He sits in the small chair, setting down the coffee cups and pouring out the bag of sugars and creams onto the table. ESTER, moving away, hiding his struggle with his vest – coincides his actions with VAL's. VAL picks up a sugar packet. He tries to tear open the packet. He almost gets it, fails. He tries again, almost gets it, and fails. This continues. Finally, disgusted, VAL tosses the sugar packet away.

VAL: Nothing / to be –

ESTER: *(Holding up a hand.)* Shhh. Not now.

> *While VAL seems to be looking away, ESTER grabs both coffee cups, tests which one is more full and sets the other one back down.*

So, where does the coffee come from today?

VAL: A coffee shop.

ESTER: Which one?

VAL: The AM/PM.

ESTER: Ugh. A gas station.

VAL: If you say so.

ESTER: Did you give them a picture?

VAL: A picture?

ESTER: Yes, a picture.

VAL: Why would I give them a picture?

ESTER stops buttoning the vest, crosses to VAL.

ESTER: Trick of the trade my lad. You offer them a picture to hang on the wall and in return they offer you free coffee.

VAL: Why would they do that?

ESTER: Because if people know that this is where true artists go to get coffee, it adds some prestige to said establishment.

VAL: Gas station.

ESTER: If you say so.

VAL: You've done this?

ESTER: But of course! I haven't paid for coffee or dry cleaning in over ten years!

VAL: But don't you have to pay for the pictures?

ESTER: Mind your own business!

VAL: Well, I did not give them a picture.

ESTER: Then, how did you get the coffee?

VAL: I didn't get the coffee.

ESTER: Then, how did *we* get the coffee?

VAL: Aunt Mary got us the coffee!

ESTER: Aunt Mary.

VAL: Aunt Mary!

ESTER: Good God, it's like she comes every night!

VAL: She does come every night. Just in case we perform. She says I'm going to be a famous actor one day!

ESTER: And you believe her?

VAL: Do you think she's lying?

ESTER: You don't have to be a liar to be crazy.

VAL: Aunt Mary is not crazy. She's just sick is all. And seeing me go on will make her feel better.

ESTER: But we *never* go on. We're the understudies. We're waiting.

VAL: Right. Well, so is Aunt Mary. Waiting for us to go on. Speaking of which, any word?

ESTER: About what?

VAL: Us.

ESTER: Us?

VAL: From him?

ESTER: Him, who?

VAL: Him, the Director.

ESTER: Oh, him! No. Nothing.

VAL: So it is not our night.

VAL returns to tasting and mixing his coffee.

ESTER: Don't say that. It could be.

VAL: How?

ESTER: This is only the matinee. Something could happen.

VAL: Don't say that. *(Beat.)* What kind of something?

ESTER: Oh, you know, the usual. A light could fall. Someone could get sick …

VAL: Or quit!

ESTER: That would never happen.

VAL: Don't say that! This is a very difficult show to do. No one even knows what it means.

ESTER goes back to trying on his vest. He fails, tries again, and fails.

ESTER: What *what* means?

VAL: The show.

ESTER: Doesn't seem so difficult to me.

VAL: Of course it's difficult. Look at you. You can't even get your costume on. Imagine if we had to go on stage.

ESTER: We never go on stage.

VAL: Don't say that! It's only the matinee! Something could happen!

Silence. ESTER continues trying on his costume. He struggles. He almost has it!

ESTER: Help!

VAL rushes behind him and tries to button the small vest.

VAL: You have to breath in.

ESTER sucks in a breath. VAL still can't get it buttoned.

VAL: I said breath in!

ESTER's face is getting red.

VAL: BREATH IN!

ESTER lets out a rush of air.

VAL: BREATH IN!

ESTER: I AM BREATHING IN!

They give up.

ESTER hangs the vest back up and looks at it suspiciously.

ESTER: It's beginning to get alarming. It fit yesterday … or was it the day before?

VAL: The day before. We were dark yesterday.

ESTER: *(Gloomily.)* I'm dark most days.

VAL: *Life's but a walking shadow, a poor player, that struts and frets his hour upon the stage, and then is heard no more; it is a tale told by an idiot, full of sound and fury, signifying nothing.*

ESTER: What?

VAL: Signifying nothing.

ESTER: What?

VAL: Signifying nothing!

ESTER: Ah… sweet *Hamlet.*

VAL: What?

ESTER: *Hamlet.*

VAL: What?

ESTER: *Hamlet.* You just quoted *Hamlet,* one of Mr. Shakespeare's greatest plays.

VAL: I don't think I did.

ESTER: You did.

VAL: I did not.

ESTER: Trust me, you did. I should know.

VAL: I wasn't quoting *Hamlet.* I was quoting *"Great Classical Monologues For Men".*

ESTER: Are you sure?

VAL: Of course I'm sure. Here, I'll do another: *And Seeing Ignorance is the Curse of God, Knowledge the wing wherewith we fly to heaven.*

ESTER: Ugh, do not speak to me of God. I gave him up years ago.

VAL: You don't believe in God?

ESTER: Of course not. I'm a devout atheist.

VAL: I thought you were a devout Catholic.

ESTER: *(Exploding.)* I don't see how they're mutually exclusive! Besides, a true artist must believe in himself above all else.

VAL: I don't agree.

ESTER: Then, you are not a true artist. Don't tell me you still believe in God?

VAL: I do believe in GOD! Good Orderly Direction! I can sum up most of my beliefs with a good acronym.

ESTER: Christ.

Beat. VAL picks up his script off the table as if rehearsing his lines.

VAL: Godot.

ESTER: What?

VAL: Godot?

ESTER: Yes?

VAL: The play. Are we saying it right? Is it Godot? Or GODot? Or maybe GOD–DOT?

ESTER: *(Uninterested.)* I have no idea.

VAL: We should figure it out, shouldn't we?

ESTER: Why?

VAL: In case we go on!

ESTER: Don't be absurd. We never go on. We're waiting.

VAL: Doesn't seem so absurd to me.

ESTER gets up and tries on his vest again. VAL returns to putting sugar and cream in his coffee. The sound of the play can be heard in the background.

Suddenly ESTER throws down his vest.

ESTER: *(Exploding.)* It wasn't always like this, you know!

VAL: Calm yourself.

ESTER: I once played *Hamlet* in a production at the park!

VAL: *Titus.*

ESTER: Whatever.

VAL: And what was it like?

ESTER: I forget. An actor must never remember lest his performance become stale.

VAL: Was it well-received?

ESTER grabs the small bust of Beethoven and holds it like some great award. He carries it with him, becoming "his": his property, his personification of himself, and his personification of all great artists.

ESTER: Oh, very! I got a mention in the program.

VAL: You always get mentioned in the program.

ESTER: I do, don't I! They said it was the best *Hamlet* that year!

VAL: *Titus.*

ESTER: Whatever. It was great! Sort of. It's never as great as you imagine.

VAL: Oh, someday I want to play *Hamlet.*

ESTER: *Titus.*

VAL: Whatever.

ESTER: Work hard, study hard, and someday you will. Look at me!

ESTER refers to the bust of Beethoven.

VAL: But, you're still waiting. We both are.

ESTER: We are a part of a very important production. I mean Beckett … you know … *Beckett.*

VAL: Who?

ESTER: Sam Beckett.

Blank stare from VAL.

ESTER: Samuel Beckett … ? The author? He's very well respected.

VAL: Is he? Do you think he'll come?

ESTER: He's dead.

VAL: Don't say that!

ESTER: My friend, he's been dead for years. They all have.

VAL: All, who?

ESTER thrusts the bust of Beethoven towards VAL.

ESTER: The greats! All the great artists! Williams, Ibsen, Chekhov … Sophocles! How I miss them.

ESTER gazes upward in memoriam. VAL joins his gaze.

VAL: Did you know them?

ESTER: No, not physically. But that's the state of things, I'm afraid. The greats are dead and have been replaced with sophomoric reinterpretations of things that have already been seen. Nothing new, nothing to be done! It's the very reason I stopped doing film!

VAL: You've never done film.

ESTER: Stopped pursuing doing film!

VAL: That's because you don't have a talent agent.

ESTER: Yet.

VAL: Yet. Why don't you have an talent agent yet?

ESTER: It's not my fault, you know. These days talent agents won't talk to you unless you are famous or unless you look like someone famous or unless someone who looks like you becomes famous. In the end, all there is to do is wait. Wait for death or a phone call, whichever comes first. And just hope someone remembers your *Hamlet*.

VAL: *Titus.*

VAL hands ESTER a coffee.

ESTER: Whatever.

They 'cheers' coffee cups and each take a sip.

VAL: That's why I got into all this, you know.

ESTER: What? Why?

VAL: To be remembered. I want people to remember me when I'm dead.

ESTER: Vanity of vanities. I'm not in this business for celebrity. I'm in it for the art. Fame and fortune be damned! I need only a stage and lines to speak. Two planks and a passion, I care not if anyone sees me.

VAL: Really?

ESTER: But, of course! An actor never needs an audience.

VAL: Why would you put on a play for no audience?

ESTER: Because the show must go on!

VAL: True. Do you think we will?

ESTER: Go on?

VAL nods.

ESTER: In this show?

VAL nods.

ESTER: Of course! Our time is nigh. The Director will want to make a change. Add some new blood to the production. As soon as he gets here, he'll tell us. You'll see.

VAL: And then we'll get our big break!

ESTER: One never knows who is in the audience.

VAL: Directors!

ESTER: Writers!

VAL: Producers!

ESTER: Press!

VAL: Aunt Mary!

ESTER gives a disgusted look.

ESTER: Ugh.

VAL: When will he get here?

ESTER: Who?

VAL: The Director.

ESTER: How should I know?

VAL: But you said he was coming tonight.

ESTER: Oh, yes. Of course, he is. I'm sure he is. I mean, he has to let us know when we'll go on. Right? I'm sure it's all been arranged.

VAL: Oh, good.

ESTER: But before that happens, we really must address some things about your technique. I've taken some notes for you. Nothing major.

ESTER sits VAL down in the chair.

ESTER: First, you're not a very good actor.

VAL: *(Offended.)* You take that back!

ESTER: You don't listen very well.

VAL: The hell did you just say?!

ESTER: And your intentions …

VAL: I'll give you until three or something's gonna something!

ESTER: A good actor …

VAL: One!

ESTER: Listens …

VAL: Two!

ESTER: But all you do –

VAL: Three!

ESTER: – is say your lines.

VAL: But, I'm supposed say my lines!

ESTER: Wrong! A good actor always listens!

VAL: But I –

ESTER: Shush!

ESTER holds up his hands for quiet as he and VAL attempt to listen.

VAL: But I don't –

ESTER: Shush!

VAL: *(Whispering.)* But I don't hear anything –

ESTER: *(Yelling.)* That's because you're not listening! This is the type of thing they're teaching at Juilliard.

VAL: You went to Juilliard?

ESTER: Of course not! No one actually goes to Juilliard! I took a workshop once. Overheard another actor talking about Juilliard and the biz.

VAL: The biz?

ESTER: Yes, our biz. The entertainment business.

VAL gives him a blank stare.

ESTER: Show business. There's a song about it. "There's no business like…"

ESTER begins to hum the song. VAL, inspired, begins a soft shoe routine while singing the song with full voice. He ends with a theatrical, but still sad, finish. ESTER hates it.

ESTER: No. That's not it.

VAL: Oh.

ESTER: Anyway, I have all kinds of great tips for the biz.

VAL: Like what?

ESTER: Okay, I'll tell you, but this information isn't free.

VAL: Oh?

ESTER: When not acting, I find it fulfilling to share my knowledge with the younger artists of our community.

VAL: You teach acting?

ESTER: Among other things! Directing, improvisation, *writing for the cinema.*

VAL: You mean screenwriting?

ESTER: If you must.

VAL: How much do you charge?

ESTER: For my level one class, three hundred.

VAL: Dollars?

ESTER: Usually. But I accept most currencies. Oh, don't worry about the money. When they see you on stage, they'll pay you four hundred a performance, at least! More than enough for you to pay for my classes!

VAL: I don't know.

ESTER: Trust me, you need them.

VAL: Well, what do I learn?

ESTER: Level one is all about the *Miserly* technique.

VAL: The what?

ESTER: *Miserly.* What you do is give as little as possible to your fellow actor by just repeating what they say over and over again.

VAL: You're just repeating what they say over and over again?

ESTER: *You're* just repeating what they say over and over again.

VAL: You're *just* repeating what they say over and over again?

ESTER: You're just *repeating* what they say over and over again.

This continues until just before the first audience member/performer vomits from repetition.

ESTER: Yes.

VAL: Yes.

ESTER: Yes.

VAL: Yes.

ESTER: YES!

This continues in the same fashion.

VAL: How does that make me better?

ESTER: I am being *miserly* with my talent, forcing you to be better with yours.

VAL: Oh … Smart. What about level two?

ESTER: Well, I don't want to give you too much, but level two is all about *Mamet*.

ESTER pronounces the name 'Mamet' with a silent 't'.

VAL: *Mamet*?

ESTER: *Mamet*. The art of swearing on stage.

VAL: But I don't like to swear.

ESTER: *(Angry.)* Then you are a son of a bitch, cock-suck mother-fuck! It's very handy for film work.

VAL: Film work? Sign me up!

ESTER: We'll begin right away!

VAL: What's first?

ESTER: Unfortunately, for you, I must require that you take my pre-level one class for beginning beginners.

VAL: Oh, really?

ESTER: Yes, you are very far behind in your training. You must still learn to be in the moment.

VAL: The moment?

ESTER: The moment.

VAL: What moment?

ESTER: The current moment. Now.

VAL: Right now?

ESTER: No, now is gone. We're talking about this moment now.

VAL: Right now?

ESTER: No. Now.

VAL: Now?

ESTER: No! We missed now!

VAL: When?

ESTER: Back then! We're dealing with now.

VAL: Now?

ESTER: Yes!

VAL: I'm in the moment?

ESTER: You're in the moment now!

VAL: I'm in the moment now!

ESTER: But now you must forget now.

VAL: Forget what now?

ESTER: Exactly. An actor must learn to forget and then forgive himself for forgetting.

VAL: So, what do we do now?

ESTER: Improvisation! The important thing about improvisation is "yes and … "

VAL: And what?

ESTER: Exactly. Just be anything. There is no wrong! Begin!

VAL looks around confused.

ESTER: Wrong! We're dealing with "yes and …"

VAL: And what?

ESTER: Yes. Follow your impulse! Support everything! Deny nothing! And begin!

Beat.

VAL makes a decision.

VAL: It sure was a rough day at the doctor's office –

ESTER: Wrong! You are a policeman and it's the happiest day of your life.

VAL: But, I'm not happy.

ESTER: Yes, you are.

VAL: No, I'm not.

ESTER: Yes, you are.

VAL: No, I'm not!

ESTER: Never argue a note! Acting is difficult. An actor never should be.

VAL: Am I a difficult actor?

VAL goes and sits again. ESTER back to the costume stand.

VAL: Do you think he noticed?

ESTER: I'm sure he did. I mean, he hasn't been by, has he?

VAL: And that's because of me?

ESTER: Your acting probably offended him.

VAL: Could be you, you know.

ESTER: No, no. It couldn't be me.

VAL: Well, at least my costume fits.

ESTER: My costume fits.

VAL: Not anymore. It doesn't fit anymore.

ESTER: Don't say that! It does fit.

VAL: It does not.

ESTER: It has to fit. It's my costume.

VAL: And yet it doesn't.

ESTER: Of course it fits. Don't be absurd.

VAL: I'm not being absurd. It doesn't fit.

ESTER: It fits because it is mine! It is mine because it fits!

VAL tries to work through that logic. Gives up. Silence.

ESTER goes back to trying on his costume. VAL sits, plays with his bowler hat.

A voice is heard off stage.

VOICE: *(OS.)* Damn! Well where the hell is it?

They both perk up.

VAL: Did you hear that?

ESTER: Yes. It sounded like a shout!

VAL: Do you think it's him?

ESTER: Him, who?

VAL: Him, the Director!

ESTER: Bah, why would he shout?

VAL: Something happened?

ESTER: You think?

VAL: He's not happy with the show.

ESTER: He's fired an actor.

VAL: In the middle of the show?

ESTER: He fired both!

VAL: You think?

ESTER: I told you! It's our time!

VAL: Aunt Mary!

They turn and look at each other and are in the same poses as they were during the Miserly exercise.

ESTER: *(Realizing.)* Oh, God! We might have to go on stage!

VAL: Finally, Aunt Mary will see our work!

ESTER: I think I might be sick!

VAL: And who knows who else is in the audience!

ESTER: My costume doesn't even fit!

VAL: Directors!

ESTER: *(To himself.)* I'm sweating ...

VAL: Producers!

ESTER: I can't...

VAL: Press!

ESTER: I've forgotten...

Beat.

VAL: The whole world could be out there!

ESTER: Oh, my God ...

VAL: Something is happening!

ESTER: *(Full panic.)* I DON'T KNOW ANY OF MY LINES!

VAL: You don't?

ESTER & VAL: PANIC!

VAL: It's alright.

ESTER: What do I do?

VAL: Calm yourself.

ESTER: WE ARE ABOUT TO GO ON, I CAN'T
REMEMBER MY LINES AND YOU TELL ME TO
CALM MYSELF?! I DON'T KNOW ANY OF MY
LINES!

VAL: Well, let's rehearse them.

ESTER: No! Let's rehearse them!

VAL: Excellent idea.

ESTER: From the beginning … begin!

A long pause.

They look out. They look at each other, look down, back to each other and back out again. They try to start a line but no words come out.

ESTER: From the beginning… Begin!

Nothing. They switch places and start again.

ESTER: From the beginning… Begin!

Nothing. They look at each other. They get mad at each other, pointing at one another, trying to physically force or urge the lines out of each other's mouths. Finally, they collapse in a heap, defeated.

ESTER: Nothing to be done!

VAL: I'm beginning to come around to that opinion!

LAURA: *(OS)* I don't know where it is! This isn't my fault!

ESTER and VAL jump up and scramble to find a place to hide. They try a few places that don't work ("Breath in!" "I am breathing in!"), eventually hiding behind the costume rack.

Enter ASSISTANT STAGE MANAGER LAURA. She is dressed in a black T-shirt, black cargo pants, black sneakers. She wears glasses and her hair is in a pony tail partially hidden under a black beret. Her T-shirt may or may not reference a renaissance fair or her favorite musical. She caries a box of props from the show and her "Waiting for Godot" technical script in a thick binder filled with sound & light cues and stage blocking written on multiple colored pages. Around her neck rests her headset. Either angry or sad, she is having a bad day.

VAL and ESTER thrust their heads out between the costumes and look at LAURA cautiously.

ESTER: *(To VAL.)* Is that him?

VAL: Who, her?

ESTER: Yes, her. Is that him?

VAL: Him who? Godot!

ESTER: Who?

VAL: You know, the play?

ESTER: No, is that him the Director?!

VAL squints and looks LAURA up and down.

VAL: Oh, him. No, I don't think so.

ESTER: How can you tell?

VAL: Well, she doesn't look like him.

ESTER: As if you know what he looks like.

VAL: We could ask him?

ESTER: Fool, you don't just ask a director a question! You must be spoken to first!

LAURA is staring at VAL and ESTER who are still hiding behind the costume rack staring at her.

VAL: Should I make a sound?

ESTER: What?

VAL: You know, to get his attention.

ESTER: Excellent idea.

They duck back down behind their hiding place.

VAL: *(Towards LAURA making a bird call.)* Whoo!... HOOT!... CAAAWWW!

They stand up in their place, in full view of LAURA. ESTER is disgusted with VAL.

ESTER: *(Directing.)* What are you doing? To be the bird, one must think as the bird! Then move and speak as the bird would move and speak!

They duck back down. VAL really commits to his performance as a bird.

VAL: CAAAAAAWWW! KAKAAAWWWW! KREEKAAAWWWKAA!

VAL bursts out of his hiding place, his performance taking him around the room in flight. ESTER follows. Exhausted VAL "lands" near ESTER.

ESTER: *(Clapping.)* Wonderful! Bravo! Capital! Very well played!

VAL: Thank you!

They embrace.

ESTER: Did you feel it? You were in the moment!

VAL: I felt something.

ESTER: My classes are paying off.

LAURA stares at them.

LAURA: There it is. Is that your vest?

ESTER steps out in front of the costume rack, nervous. He looks to VAL and signals for him to come out.

LAURA: Well?

ESTER: Are you speaking to us, sir?

LAURA: What?

ESTER: Are you speaking to us?

LAURA: Who else would I be speaking to?

VAL: *(Clapping.)* Oh, thank you, sir! An honor!

LAURA: What?

VAL: I'm sorry.

LAURA: Well?

VAL: What?

LAURA: Is it?

VAL: Yes?

LAURA: Is it your vest?

ESTER: Who?

VAL: I'm not wearing a vest.

LAURA: I wasn't talking to you.

VAL: Thank you.

VAL escapes to hide.

LAURA: Is that your vest or not?

ESTER points across the room.

ESTER: Look out!

As LAURA turns away, ESTER tries to hide against the wall in plain sight. It does not work.

LAURA: No, the one on your body that doesn't fit you?

ESTER looks at his vest, embarrassed.

ESTER: Why do you ask?

LAURA: Estragon is missing his vest. He's been doing the whole first act in a vest twice his size. There might have been a mix up. Is that one yours?

ESTER: Of course, it is mine. Why it fits perfectly.

VAL: Well, no, it doesn't –

ESTER: *(To VAL.)* Quiet, you idiot! First they take your costume, then they take your part!

VAL: They do?

LAURA: Are you sure it's yours?

ESTER: Quite. Are you … you know?

LAURA: Am I who?

VAL: The Director.

LAURA: Oh, God, no.

ESTER: *(To VAL.)* I told you it wasn't him …

LAURA: I look nothing like her.

VAL: Her?

LAURA turns and begins cleaning up clutter, putting away props while searching for the vest.

ESTER: *(Laughing embarrassed.)* Of course *her*, you buffoon. Women make excellent directors. Everyone knows this. *(To LAURA.)* My colleague, he is new to the biz.

LAURA: What biz?

ESTER: Why, the entertainment business, of course.

LAURA: Is that what this is?

ESTER: *(Laughing embarrassed.)* Exactly.

Beat.

ESTER steps behind forcing VAL to be front and center.

VAL: Do you know who we are?

LAURA: Of course.

ESTER & VAL look at each other and LAURA with suspicion.

ESTER: A fan?

VAL: We have a fan?

ESTER: We probably have more than one.

VAL: You think?

ESTER: Word has spread that we are involved with this production. Quick! Find out more about her.

VAL turns to LAURA, inches forward, nervous.

VAL: So, do you come to the theatre often?

LAURA: I'm here every night.

VAL: *(To ESTER.)* She's here every night!

VAL turns back to LAURA.

VAL: *(To LAURA.)* Why are you here every night?

LAURA: I work here.

VAL: *(To ESTER.)* She says she works here.

ESTER gives him a confused look.

VAL: *(To LAURA.)* Are you sure?

LAURA: I'm the ASM.

VAL: She says she's the ASM.

ESTER: Idiot.

ESTER hits VAL with his hat, shoving VAL out of the way.

ESTER: Of course, the assistant stage manager!

ESTER offers a theatrical bow to LAURA.

ESTER: We meet so many people … er … fans back here my colleague gets confused. Wonderful to see you again, Lisa. Lonna.

LAURA: Laura.

ESTER: Lama?

LAURA: Laura.

ESTER: Lama. I'm a huge fan of what you people…

LAURA: Huh?

ESTER: *(Recovering.)* I'm a very large admirer of what … We are actors … players, if you will, in the cast of …

LAURA: *Waiting For* –

ESTER: *Waiting for Godot.*

LAURA: I know. We all are.

ESTER: Isn't that the truth.

VAL: How is it out there, on stage? How is the performance?

LAURA: It is what it is.

VAL: Maybe the second act will be better?

LAURA: Won't make a difference.

VAL: Maybe it's the acting. Perhaps if two other actors were to step in the production would be…

LAURA: No. The acting is acting. They have no idea what the play is about.

ESTER: No one does.

LAURA: Everyone does.

ESTER: It is a mystery.

LAURA: *(Realizing.)* Oh, you're a crazy person.

ESTER: Or am I just typecast that way?

LAURA: Are you saying you're a crazy person because you've been cast as a crazy person?

ESTER: Chicken or the egg, Lama.

LAURA: *(To VAL.)* Are you as crazy as he is?

VAL: Me? I wish. Aunt Mary seems to think if I just keep at it –

ESTER: Stop talking about that lunatic.

VAL: She is not a lunatic! She says I'll be a famous actor one day if I just –

ESTER: *(Cutting VAL off.)* He has potential, I'll grant you that. But he is very green.

LAURA begins to leave, still holding her prop box and script.

LAURA: I'm sure it will all work out for you. Acting is not that hard.

ESTER: What?! How dare you! What?!

LAURA: Well, it isn't. You wear a costume someone else made, you stand where someone else tells you to, and then you say lines someone else wrote. What's the big deal?

ESTER: *(Flabbergasted.)* What is the big deal?! Actors breath the breath of life into those characters – creating, for a short time, the existence of a person who only lived on paper but a moment ago! We are the conduits of creative inspiration!

VAL: It's very hard work.

LAURA: Looks like it.

LAURA starts to leave again.

ESTER: Madam, allow me to give you a brief example of one of the many steps it takes to create a character.

ESTER stands center stage.

ESTER: In this exercise, the actor will choose an animal that best represents the spirit of his character.

ESTER stretches, preparing his instrument

ESTER: This is a classic tool for actors! I shall *be*come a gorilla! Not unlike Brando as he prepared for *Streetcar*! And … begin!

Instantly, ESTER becomes a Brando-esq Gorilla, pounding his chest and performing bits from A Streetcar Named Desire, *and then memorable bits from other Brando movies, and then memorable bits from movies not starring Brando:* Star Wars, A Few Good Men, *etc. VAL & LAURA watch. Finally, ESTER, exhausted, finishes.*

ESTER: *(Out of breath.)* And… Acting! You see? True art is a challenge both of the mind and the body. I master my instrument and use it to tell the story.

LAURA: So, how does jumping around like a gorilla help you as an understudy?

ESTER: It is the very spine of my character!

LAURA: A gorilla?

ESTER: I am always a gorilla!

LAURA: Whatever.

LAURA begins to leave.

ESTER: Oh, well! We'd love to see the *assistant* stage manager attempt something as difficult as acting.

LAURA turns back, angry.

LAURA: I help call a show! That's difficult! Acting is easy. They let anyone do it!

ESTER: Well, ahoy then! We'd love to see you attempt something from your script while we watch you act your big stupid foot right in to your big stupider mouth. En Guard!

LAURA gets up on the chair, opens her script, and re-adjusts her head set. She begins to read the stage directions. VAL and ESTER are captivated.

LAURA: "ESTER STEPS DOWN CENTER STAGE RIGHT LOOKING OUT TO THE AUDIENCE. STAND BY LIGHT QUE 27.

"Time. Life. That's what happened. Passed me by, long ago, I suppose and I've been living a lie,"

LIGHT QUE 27 GO

"shoveling bullshit right along with all the other bullshit shovelers."

LIGHT FADE SINGLE ON ESTER. VAL MOVES DOWN CENTER STAGE LEFT. STAND BY LIGHT QUE 28.

"And this is what my life has become. Devoted to my own cause and not to the cause bigger than myself."

LIGHT CUE 28 GO. STAND BY LIGHT CUE 29.

"Art. That terrible whore. And now she has left me in the ditch where I await death."

LIGHT CUE 29 GO.

VAL claps, inspired.

VAL: What's that from?

LAURA: The second act.

ESTER: Is it?

LAURA: Acting is only one part of the show, a part anyone can do. Managing the show is far more difficult, especially when you're forced to deal with actors acting like actors. The acting in this show is so simple deaf puppets using sign language could perform it!

LAURA steps off the chair and tries to leave.

VAL: That's brilliant!

ESTER: That's dreadful.

VAL: Oh, I wish we were doing that!

ESTER: Deaf puppets?! That doesn't make any sense.

VAL: Of course, it does! Think about it! Deaf puppets implies several truths about our existence. One, we're all just dangling on strings controlled by fate or God or the universe, none of us having actual free will. Deafness expresses our inability to address the pain of life and our own mortality. And sign language for puppets would be almost impossible to understand which would further emphasize how the human race really is just a bunch of deaf, blind creatures incapable of truly understanding each other while we wait around to die! I mean, Beckett could hardly express it better!

ESTER: That's absurd.

VAL: Exactly.

LAURA looks at VAL, impressed. VAL, excited about his epiphany, looks back at her.

VAL: "We have time to grow old."

LAURA: We do, don't we. You know that's the kind of stuff they are teaching at Juilliard.

ESTER: Bah! What do you know about Juilliard?

LAURA: My cousin went to Juilliard.

ESTER: Nope. No. I don't think so. No one actually goes to Juilliard.

VAL & ESTER share a laugh.

LAURA: How would you possibly know that?

ESTER: Because I am an educator of theatre.

LAURA: You teach theatre?

VAL: Amongst other things.

LAURA: Sounds like someone doesn't have a talent agent.

ESTER: Yet! I am waiting for the right representation for me! Once I have a talent agent, it'll be smooth sailing from there on out! I'll be working until I don't want to work any more! Oh yes! I won't even have to audition once I have a talent agent. They'll just make a call and I'm in! A guaranteed career! It's the Blue Ox to Easy Street on the sunny side, as they say.

LAURA: No one says that.

ESTER: I just said that.

VAL: Excuse me. How do I get a talent agent?

LAURA: There are talent agents everywhere.

ESTER and VAL look around suspiciously.

LAURA: Odds are you'll be pissing next to one in the bathroom.

ESTER: Ugh, so vulgar for a lady.

LAURA: The question is, would a talent agent want you?

LAURA directs her gaze at VAL.

LAURA: Well, this has been interesting. I just needed to check on that vest and let you know we're at intermission.

ESTER: Is the Director coming?

LAURA: No.

ESTER: But, maybe later?

LAURA: No.

VAL: Did the Director say anything about us?

LAURA: No. We're at ten now.

As LAURA exits STAGE LEFT.

ESTER: Thank you, ten.

VAL: Thank you, ten.

ESTER: The nerve of that child. Coming back here to check on my vest! They're trying to get rid of me!

VAL: Is she right?

ESTER: About what?

VAL: Acting being easy and finding a talent agent. All that stuff.

ESTER: Don't you listen to her! Don't you listen to her for one moment! This town is full of people like that. Angry about their lot in life, so they come back stage and talk to true artists about their vests!

VAL: Huh?

ESTER: She is trying to get rid of us! I know it! Don't listen to her. She doesn't know a damn thing about the biz! Went to Juilliard, please, as if anyone ever has!

VAL: But do you think a talent agent will want me?

ESTER: Of course! Probably. Maybe. Who knows? You're so new! It takes a long time to establish oneself in this industry.

Silence.

Just do as I do, and when the time is right, you will no doubt have an agent. You have to pay your dues, you know. We must suffer for our art.

ESTER slowly returns to trying on his vest. VAL goes back to sitting and sipping his coffee.

VAL: Should we leave?

ESTER: No. That wouldn't be right.

VAL: Why? No one cares.

ESTER: Someone does. Your Aunt Martha.

VAL: Mary.

ESTER: Whatever. She cares.

VAL: She's not going to see us.

ESTER: Don't say that. You mustn't give up hope. We could still go on!

VAL: How?

ESTER: It's only the matinee. Something could happen!

VAL: Like what?

ESTER: A light could fall, someone could get sick, or someone could get fired.

VAL: That won't happen. Not by tonight.

ESTER: You don't know that.

VAL: Not unless somebody makes something happen.

ESTER: Well, what if we made something happen?

VAL: What are you talking about?

ESTER: We could curse them.

VAL: Huh?

ESTER: Curse them. Put a hex on them.

VAL: You're an atheist. You don't believe in hexes.

ESTER: Not a witch hex. I mean an old theatre hex. You know, where you're not suppose to say a certain *(Whisper.)* Scottish play unless you're doing it.

VAL: Oh, you mean Mac –

ESTER covers his mouth.

ESTER: Yes! That's what I mean!

VAL: Or, we could wish them luck. You know, you're supposed to say break a leg, but instead, we say "*good luck.*"

They look about to see if anyone heard them. They giggle to each other.

ESTER: Let's do it!

VAL: What do you think will happen?

ESTER: Anything!

ESTER: Look! They took it. Any minute now they'll come back here and take my soul. I've been cut.

ESTER sits defeated in the chair. VAL stands across from him.

VAL: Cut?

ESTER: From the show. I'm finished in this town.

VAL: What do you mean?

ESTER: Don't cry for me.

VAL: I'm not crying.

ESTER: I'll never perform on stage again.

VAL: You've been fired?

ESTER: I'm just another out-of-work actor who couldn't hack it.

VAL: From this show?

ESTER: I'm humiliated.

VAL: You're getting fired from this show?

ESTER: I guess I don't have the talent after all.

VAL: What on earth are you talking about?

ESTER: I'll just go on teaching, I suppose.

VAL: But why would they cut you?

ESTER: Those who can, do. And those who can't...

VAL: So, you're done?

ESTER: I'm finished. They've slammed the door shut on me. This show was to be my big break! This was going to finally show the world just what kind of actor I was. A few good reviews here and soon word would spread. After a couple of months, the calls would come. A run in Chicago. Then, New York. A modest run off-Broadway, and then ... Broadway!

ESTER, lost in his dream, 'performs' his monologue. He finds a lit floor lamp, tips it forward so the light hits him like a spotlight from below. Somewhere in the distance, lonely film noir music plays. Maybe he pulls out an electronic cigarette and smokes it dramatically as he speaks.

ESTER: And after the Tony nod, I would start taking offers. Offers for film. Serious roles. Something sexy and cool. It would be charming but dangerous. Really make people think, you know, about Africa … Or wherever. And then, people would know me. They'd think of me when they looked at the trouble in their own life and thank God I was there to tell their story. I was to be the noble artist whom everyone loved. And I would no longer rent. For I would own.

VAL: But, what happened?

ESTER: Time. Life. That's what happened. Passed me by long ago, I suppose, and I've been living a lie, shoveling bullshit right along with all the other bullshit shovelers.

And this is what my life has become. Devoted to my own cause and not to the cause bigger than myself. Art. That terrible whore.

And now she has left me in the ditch where I await death.

VAL: No, I mean what happened during intermission?

The music cuts out suddenly and ESTER lets go of the lamp, killing the "spotlight".

ESTER: They took my vest! It's gone! I have no character! They've fired me. They've killed me. Later someone will come and run me out on a rail, humiliated, covered in tar and feathers. They took my vest! And it was all I had.

VAL: I took your vest.

Beat.

ESTER: What?

VAL: I took your vest.

ESTER: You took my vest?!

VAL: Yes, but that's not –

ESTER: You took my vest!

VAL: Yes.

ESTER: Are you working for them?

VAL: Them, who?

ESTER: The Director!

VAL: No! Well, yes, in a way. I mean, we both are.

ESTER: So, you are my replacement.

VAL: What? No! What?

ESTER: This business! This industry! So cruel! They take the ones you love and turn them against you!

ESTER starts to stalk VAL.

VAL: I'm not –

ESTER: You performed my role at some sort of secret audition, didn't you?! Probably in this very theatre, in a dirty, back room.

VAL: We're in the dirty, back room.

ESTER: They promised you fame and fortune if you would only betray your best friend.

VAL: Well, I wouldn't call us best –

ESTER begins to pack up his "belongings". He takes the bust of Beethoven, one of the lamps, a coat rack, and starts to walk off stage.

ESTER: You did all kinds of sexual favors for them, I suppose? And who could blame you? This was the opportunity of a lifetime. What you did, you did for art and personal gain. Do not feel ashamed. It's the American way. My God, what has happened to this great country of ours?!

Beat.

VAL: I'm not your replacement!

ESTER: You're not my replacement?

VAL: I'm not your replacement. How would I replace you?

He begins to walk across STAGE LEFT, lost in his own ego, he unpacks his "belongings" to where they were.

ESTER: Of course, how *could* you replace me? Me, a true artist ...

VAL: I'm already cast as an understudy, so that wouldn't make any sense.

ESTER: They would never replace me with someone like you.

VAL: What's that supposed to mean?

ESTER: I'm not being fired!

ESTER: My inner artist is sensitive. I really can't control its temperament you know. Few true artists can. It's a curse. And yet, it's what drives us to greatness.

VAL: That's some ego you have there. You were just about ready to kill yourself over nothing. I don't think it's very healthy going from the highs to the lows like you do.

ESTER: I mean, the whole idea is just silly when you think of it. Why would they replace *me* with *you*? In truth, I've always felt the person best suited to replace me would have been Olivier, or maybe Burton. But alas, they have left this mortal coil.

VAL: Your vest is not what I wanted to talk about. I have some very big news to share. News that's more important than your vest. But that doesn't matter, because it's not about you.

ESTER: Jealousy. It was a desperate grab. That's why you stole my vest.

VAL: Sorry. It was a mistake. I didn't mean to take your vest.

46

ESTER turns to VAL angry once more.

ESTER: You stole my vest.

VAL: That's not the point.

ESTER: You stole my vest.

VAL: I didn't steal your vest.

ESTER: You stole my vest.

VAL: Fine, I stole your vest.

ESTER: You stole my vest.

VAL: I stole your vest.

ESTER: You stole my vest.

VAL: I stole – No! Not this again!

ESTER stares down VAL.

ESTER: Return my character's property!

ESTER begins to chase VAL around the stage. VAL tries to fend him off. It turns into a sad wrestle as VAL tries to take off the vest and ESTER tries to take it from him.

VAL: Wait!

ESTER: Ahoy!

VAL: Stop!

ESTER: A sad grapple!

VAL: Something happened!

ESTER: You're lucky I didn't call the authorities.

VAL: What authorities?

ESTER: The Authorities of the Stage! For it is not just my vest you stole BUT the vest of Estragon! The VEST OF BECKETT!

47

VAL: Something else more important happened!

ESTER: You nearly derailed my career! What could be more important than that?!

VAL: I got an agent!

They stop moving. ESTER has VAL in a strange version of a half nelson. Silence.

ESTER: What do you mean you got an agent?

VAL: I mean, I signed with a talent agent! From a talent agency!

ESTER releases VAL.

ESTER: You were gone fifteen minutes.

VAL: I know! I got signed across the board.

ESTER: What does that mean?

VAL: I have no idea!

ESTER: How?

VAL: How what?

ESTER: How did they … discover you?

VAL: I was pissing!

ESTER: Explain.

VAL: Well, during the intermission, I had to go to the bathroom but you were in the bathroom back here. So I went to the lobby.

ESTER: You're not supposed to do that! The lobby bathroom is for patrons of the theatre! Not the players!

VAL: I know, but you were in our bathroom and I really had to go, so I figured, why not? No one will notice.

ESTER: But someone did notice.

VAL: Exactly. So I was still wearing your vest when –

ESTER: Why *were* you wearing my vest?

VAL: Not important. It's very nice in the lobby bathroom. They have towels!

ESTER: They have towels?!

VAL: Yes. So, I go to the urinals.

ESTER: They have urinals?!

VAL: Yes. And as I'm pissing, I notice someone is looking at me.

ESTER: They have someone to look at you?!

VAL: Yes, and as I'm pissing a man in the bathroom asks if I'm an actor. I said, "I am." He said I looked like an actor. He asked if I was in this production. I said I was. Then he said he is a talent agent who represents talented actors across the board and was wondering if I'd like to sign. He said I had a great commercial look.

ESTER: I have a great commercial look! Has he seen me?!

VAL: I don't know. Have you gone to the bathroom?

ESTER: How did you get signed?

VAL: Oh, well I finished pissing and signed with him. Just so!

ESTER: Just so?

ESTER mimics the pissing. VAL shrugs.

VAL: Isn't it great?! Someone thought I looked like a talented actor! And that someone is a talent agent! A talent agent wanted me! Me!

ESTER: Well I suppose it's fine if you want to be the type of actor who cuts corners.

VAL: What do you mean?

ESTER: Well, it's not exactly following the rules.

VAL: What rules?

ESTER: The rule about using the lobby bathroom. Using it to get ahead. That's not exactly following the rules, my friend.

VAL: But that's not a real rule.

ESTER: Are you allowed to use the lobby bathroom?

VAL: No.

ESTER: Then, that's a real rule. You can't cheat to get ahead in this business. THERE ARE NO SHORT CUTS. We all must pay our dues. We all must suffer for our art. We all must follow the rules.

VAL: Well, maybe we shouldn't follow the rules.

ESTER: What?! How dare you! What?!

VAL: We've been following the rules and what has it gotten us?

ESTER: A fulfilling career!

ESTER thrusts the bust of Beethoven towards VAL as proof.

VAL: That isn't fulfilling. That's Beethoven!

ESTER: But we're part of a very important production, aren't we?

VAL: But look what happened the one time I didn't follow the rule.

ESTER looks lost.

VAL: I got a talent agent! And that was just by going to the bathroom! Imagine what else is out there! In other bathrooms! We should do something else. Something bold. Something rash! We should quit!

ESTER: Quit?!

VAL: Yes.

ESTER: Just walk away?!

VAL: Sure!

ESTER: Throw our responsibilities out the window?

VAL: Why not?

ESTER: We made a commitment.

VAL: Yes, but it's not working. All we're doing is waiting. And if it doesn't go anywhere, what's the point?

ESTER: What's the point of anything? It's what we do. Best not think about it.

VAL: But I want more than this. I don't want to wait.

ESTER: Oh! Well, I'm afraid you'll just have to Mr. Bathroom Pisser! There are no short cuts! We all must suffer for our art! We all must pay our dues! We all must wait for *Waiting for Godot!*

ESTER grabs his vest and goes back to trying it on by the costume rack. VAL sits down. Silence.

VAL: *(Thinking.)* Who is he do you think?

ESTER: Who is who?

VAL: Godot? You ever wonder that?

ESTER: Who is Godot?

VAL: Yes.

ESTER: No. Who is Godot?

VAL: Yeah, that's what I'm asking.

ESTER: And I'm asking you, who the hell are you talking about?

VAL: Who is Godot, the guy we're waiting for?

ESTER: We're waiting for the director.

VAL: Yes, I know. But, in the play it is who we are waiting for. And I'm asking, who is Godot? Why are we, or they, waiting for him? Is he God? Does he represent some sort of fatherly approval? Is he an abstract thing, like an ideal? Some sort of purpose maybe, or good news? Or, is he the carrot dangling on the end of a stick. A threat or an empty promise. Because he doesn't come in the end. He does not come. What kind of people hang around waiting for a promise that doesn't come?

ESTER: *(Deep in thought.)* I want you to listen to me very carefully. I have no idea what you are talking about. But I am trying to focus on my character's wants, so if you could just please be quiet …

ESTER stands at the rack and stares at the hanger that once held his vest. Silence.

VAL: You're mad that I got a talent agent.

ESTER: OF COURSE I'M MAD! Who the hell are you? What have you done? What have you accomplished? You're brand new to this business. You haven't paid your dues. Why should you get a break while we hardworking, true artists have to suffer.

VAL: I thought you were supposed to suffer for your art.

ESTER: Not me! You! You are supposed to suffer. I've suffered enough! I've been suffering for years! And I hate it. I hate all this suffering! There is nothing noble about being rejected every day for your art. Having to pull yourself up like a lackey and say, "Well, I guess I wasn't meant to have that job!" As if there is meaning to any of this! I mean, look at him! What did he do? He walked into the mens' room, relieved himself, and he got signed by a talent agent?! Where is the sense, the logic, the art in that? I can piss! Look, I can do it right now! Why not me? Call that agent!

ESTER grabs one of the coffee cups, takes it back, turns UPSTAGE and begins to piss into the coffee cup. VAL is horrified.

ESTER: Let him know I can piss on command! Critics have reviewed my piss and said, "Why, it's the best piss in town!"

ESTER sets the coffee down again.

VAL: You pissed in my coffee.

ESTER: You've been pissing in mine since the day I met you.

Silence. ESTER sits down next to the costume rack. VAL sits at his chair by the two coffee cups. Slowly, he pushes the piss cup away from him.

VAL: You and I are the only ones really doing it, you know.

ESTER: Must you go on like this?

VAL: I mean, isn't that what he's saying?

ESTER: Who?

VAL: The writer. Beckett … *Beckett!* Isn't he saying that about life and everything? That all we do is wait? We have time to grow old. We should leave.

ESTER: We can't.

VAL: Why not? No one even knows we're here. And if we're like the story, then we should just leave.

ESTER: What if something happens?

VAL: Don't say that.

VAL runs away, exiting towards the lobby. ESTER sits, in a sad, pathetic silence, alone.

VAL enters and when ESTER sees him, he is happy again.

Something like what?

ESTER: A light could fall. Someone could get sick. Someone could get fired.

VAL: Then, they'd need us.

ESTER: And, we'd get to perform.

VAL: Finally, the world will see our talent.

ESTER: It would make our careers.

VAL: Thunderous applause.

ESTER: Curtain calls.

VAL: Great reviews.

ESTER: Money.

VAL: Fame.

ESTER: Fortune.

　　We can't go!

VAL: I don't want to leave!

They embrace, excited. They stand expectantly. Slowly, the excitement dies down. ESTER moves back to the costume rack. He begins trying on his costume again. VAL eventually sits again, playing with his hat.

VAL: Do you ever have doubts?

ESTER: Doubts?

VAL: Yes, doubts.

ESTER: Doubts about what?

VAL: About yourself? About being an actor? About missing out on those things. You know, those things in life?

ESTER: Never! Wait, what things?

VAL: You know, those things. Those nice things people have in their lives. Like a house for a family.

ESTER slowly sits down on the ground, defeated, as they doubt.

VAL: A washer and dryer. A car that doesn't break down.

ESTER: Food.

VAL: A refrigerator full of food.

ESTER: Christ, I haven't eaten a meal I paid for in three months.

VAL: A wife and kids.

ESTER: The soup kitchen at Saint Mark's is not terrible.

VAL: You know, the only compliment I've ever gotten in my career was from my sister. She said she was proud of me for "really sticking with it." She has three kids, a house, and vacations with her husband in Europe.

ESTER: I keep packets of Tartar sauce in my coat pockets and I don't know why.

VAL: I've never been to Europe.

ESTER: TARTAR!

VAL: I don't want to quit acting but this is my life we're talking about. And when I die, will I look back and regret all this?

ESTER: I never got to see my nephews grow up.

VAL: My mom still pays for my plane tickets home for Christmas.

ESTER: I've never been home for Christmas. I'm Jewish.

VAL pats an emotional ESTER on the shoulder.

ESTER: What are we doing? Wait! What are we doing?! Stand up! STAND UP!

ESTER pulls VAL to his feet.

ESTER: We are actors, sir! Professional artists! We live for creative purpose, not material wealth! The bravery of what we do for the world every day makes us heroes. For we are the men in the arena, our faces dirty with blood and grime! We fail some times and succeed others, but we always get back up and keep trying. That's what makes us different from those people out there. Those people with the houses and refrigerators full of delicious, delicious food! We do what those people cannot. We create. They consume. We are the mirror to their world. Through us, they see and understand their life better. And if you can't find solace in that, then go be a bookstore clerk or a school teacher or an office manager somewhere in the middle of the country. And leave acting to those who do not care for such things.

VAL: Yeah, I guess.

ESTER: Guess nothing. Know. Be. That is what we do. What would Mr. Shakespeare think of this defeatist talk?

VAL: He wouldn't like it.

ESTER: Damn right! Stand tall, man! Visualize what you want to happen and it will! Do you see yourself failing?

VAL: No.

ESTER: What do you see then?!

VAL closes his eyes and dramatically looks out.

VAL: I see me. Myself. On stage performing *Waiting for Godot.*

ESTER: When?

VAL: Tonight!

ESTER: And the audience?

VAL: They love it. They're moved. They laugh, they cry, they are overjoyed!

ESTER: So it's not this audience.

VAL: And there is Aunt Mary! She is so happy for me!

ESTER: Alright, what else?

VAL: She is healthy! I think my performance healed her!

ESTER: Okay, open your eyes. That's just ridiculous. What are you, Jesus Christ? You can't heal –

LAURA's voice comes over the intercom.

LAURA: *(OS)* Actors, please exit the stage. Actors, please exit the stage. Ladies and Gentlemen, our apologies. We have a medical emergency in the house. If you would please quietly leave the theatre through the exit doors. Our sincerest apologies.

ESTER and VAL freeze, staring at the speaker, unsure what all this means.

LAURA enters. She begins to clean up barely giving VAL and ESTER any notice.

LAURA: The show is over guys, go home.

ESTER: A show is never over. Actors simply stop performing it.

LAURA: Well, the actors have stopped performing it tonight, and the audience is leaving.

VAL: Why?

LAURA: There was a medical emergency in the theatre; and the actors, out of respect, have decided not to finish the show.

ESTER: We'll go on!

VAL: Yes, we're ready!

LAURA: No, the audience is leaving.

ESTER: Well, get them back! This is why we are here!

LAURA: What?

VAL: Yes! We're the understudies. If the actors have left, it's up to us to finish the show!

LAURA: No. No show tonight. There was a death.

VAL: On stage?

LAURA: No, not on stage. In the house. An audience member died.

VAL: Who died?

LAURA: She was an older woman.

VAL: An older woman?

LAURA: She's here every night. We know she wasn't a donor, because no one knew her name. The paramedic said her name was –

VAL: Mary?

LAURA: Yes. Did you know her?

VAL: Aunt Mary?

LAURA: I'm sorry.

VAL: I have to leave.

VAL starts to walk off stage.

ESTER: Comrade, be brave. The show is not over.

LAURA: The show is over.

ESTER: The show is not over.

LAURA: I said, the show is over.

ESTER: The show is not over!

LAURA: Why wouldn't the show be over?

ESTER: Because the show must go on.

LAURA: No, it doesn't.

ESTER: Yes, it does!

LAURA: No, it doesn't.

ESTER: Yes, it does!

LAURA: Why does the show have to go on?

ESTER: Because it is a written rule of the theatre!

LAURA: Where is it written?

ESTER: Somewhere! Please! Please, the show must go on.

VAL looks to ESTER

VAL: She wanted to see me perform.

ESTER: And she will. She knew we were here.

LAURA begins to put things away for the night.

VAL: It was her death that will allow us to perform?

ESTER: What a gift to be given.

VAL: It's so beautiful.

ESTER: This is our something. Our something finally happened.

VAL starts to move back towards ESTER.

VAL: A light didn't fall.

ESTER: No one was fired.

VAL: No one quit.

ESTER and VAL are now CENTER STAGE.

VAL: I didn't want it to happen like this.

ESTER: No one did.

VAL: She died.

ESTER: Nothing to be done.

LAURA: Stop it! I'm not going to allow this –

LAURA steps towards VAL.

ESTER: Step away from the artist! This is our something! This
  is how it happened. A seemingly random act that fulfills
  the purpose of those who are ready when the time calls.

*VAL looks at LAURA with sympathy, and pulls away from her,
choosing ESTER.*

LAURA: Whatever.

ESTER: My friend, are you ready? Shall we show this audience
  what sacrifice is all about?

VAL: Yes. I am ready.

*LAURA exits, shutting off the lights as she goes, leaving ESTER and
VAL standing center stage in the dark.*

ESTER: Well? Shall we say our lines?

VAL: From the beginning?

ESTER: Begin!

ESTER and VAL step forward, looking out and try to say their first lines. They can't. They look at each other.

Blackout. End of Play.

GLOSSARY OF CHANGES FROM THE 2016 UK PRODUCTION.

US	UK
Bathroom	Toilet
Lobby	Foyer
Vest	Waistcoat
Talent Agent	Agent
Julliard	RADA
Intermission	Interval
Ten Minute Call	Five Minute Call
Refrigerator	Fridge
Vacations	Holidays
Plane Tickets	Train Tickets
Soup Kitchen	Food Bank
Europe	Thailand
Donor	Trustee
Gas Station	Petrol Station
Sick	Not Well
Dollars	Pounds
The AM/PM	Wild Bean
Down Centre Stage Right	Downstage Right
Down Centre Stage Left	Downstage Left
Light Cue	LXQ
Single	Spot Light
Guy	Actor
Chicago	London
Off West End	St James's Theatre
Broadway	West End
Or Wherever	Refugees
American	British

WWW.OBERONBOOKS.COM

Follow us on www.twitter.com/@oberonbooks
& www.facebook.com/OberonBooksLondon

QUARTER LIFE CRISIS

Yolanda Mercy

QUARTER LIFE CRISIS

OBERON BOOKS
LONDON

WWW.OBERONBOOKS.COM

First published in 2017 by Oberon Books Ltd
521 Caledonian Road, London N7 9RH
Tel: +44 (0) 20 7607 3637 / Fax: +44 (0) 20 7607 3629
e-mail: info@oberonbooks.com
www.oberonbooks.com

A catalogue record for this book is available from the British
Library.

PB ISBN: 9781786823564
E ISBN: 9781786823571

Cover design by Rebecca Pitt

Cover photography by The Other Richard

Visit www.oberonbooks.com to read more about all our books and to buy
them. You will also find features, author interviews and news of any author
events, and you can sign up for e-newsletters so that you're always first to
hear about our new releases.

For Mum, Letitia, Dad, Grandma Janet, Uncle Robert and Nile.

To my ancestors who battled and overcame adversity to make sure that I am here and able to share this story. This is for us.

Special thanks

Gemma Lloyd for always being supportive and helping to produce my plays.

Lola Alade, Directors Charitable Foundation, Mobius, Akili Ajibode, Anne Mulleners, Matthew Gardner, Sam Evans, Stella Kanu, Owen Calvert-Lyons, Soho Theatre, Mope Bello, Uncle Wale, Bas, Barbara Palczynski, Creative Society, The British Council, Simeilia Hodge-Dallaway, Old Vic New Voices, Tamasha, Dreda Say Mitchell, Tony, Jamie D Hunt, Reuben, Jules Orcullo, Sophie Flack, Omari Brown, Nadine Gray, Georgia Dodsworth, Alex, Sacha, Holly Gallagher, Rachel Moore, and the shadow assistant directors.

Our wonderful crowdfunder supporters: Stephanie Owens, Rob Ellis, Jonathan Wakeham, Abiola Onike, Shivuan Woolfson, Susanne, Mehnaz Khan, Nathan Adabadze, Sophie, Emma Forth, Julienne Orcullo, Benzi Benzington, Christopher Haydon, Laura Chetty, Yoshi E.A., Kaysha Woollery, Hammed Animashaun, Ahazad Khalid, Estelle Papadimitriou, Jamie Hunt, Mofya, Simon Gibbons, and anonymous givers.

Lucy and Oberon Books for taking a risk on a new writer and providing me with my first publishing deal.

And everyone who has supported me along the way.

Quarter Life Crisis was first previewed at Arc Stockton on 12th April 2017 and OvalHouse Theatre on 13th April 2017. Full production premiere at Underbelly (Cowgate) on 3rd August 2017.

ALICIA performed by Yolanda Mercy

Writer	Yolanda Mercy
Director	Jade Lewis
Producer	Yolanda Mercy and Jade Lewis
Dramaturg	Jules Haworth
Rehearsal and Production Photography	Helen Murray

Actor and Writer – Yolanda Mercy

Yolanda trained at the Brit School, Laban, and Central School of Speech and Drama. She is the Underbelly Untapped Award recipient 2017, Artist to Watch 2017 by the British Council and Associate Artist at OvalHouse. Her writing has also been featured in Huffington Post.

Actor credits include: *On The Edge of Me* (Soho Theatre & UK tour); *The Street Scene* (Young Vic); *Bow Down* (The Opera Group); *The Kilburn Passion* (Tricycle Theatre) and *Aladdin* (Lyric Hammersmith).

Writing credits include: *On The Edge of Me* (Soho Theatre & UK tour); *Divide and Rule* (National Theatre Studio); *His Life Matters* (The Bush) and *Gods of Atlantis* (St James Theatre).

Director – Jade Lewis

Jade is a Creative Associate at The Gate and recipient of the Boris Karloff Award.

Directing credits include: *a profoundly affectionate, passionate devotion to someone (-noun)* (Royal Court); *The Convert* (The Gate); *5 Years Down the Line* (National Theatre Studio); *On The Edge of Me* (Soho Theatre & UK Tour); *Followers* (Southwark Playhouse); *Venus/Mars* (The Bush) and *Blackta* (Young Vic).

Dramaturg – Jules Haworth

Jules is Education Producer at Soho Theatre. She is part of Soho Theatre's Artistic team, considering new plays and shows for the stage and running workshops for young and emerging artists.

As a dramaturg Jules has worked on shows including: *Brute* by Izzy Tennyson (Ideas Tap Underbelly Award 2015, Underbelly); *Muscovado* by Matilda Ibini (Alfred Fagon Award 2015, Theatre 503); *Villain* by Martin Murphy (Offie Nomination 2017, Edinburgh Fringe Festival); *On the Edge of Me* by Yolanda Mercy (Soho Theatre & UK Tour) and *Dust* by Milly Thomas (The Stage Edinburgh Award 2017).

Quarter Life Crisis was originally created with the generous support of Arts Council England, Peggy Ramsay Foundation, OvalHouse Theatre and Arc Stockton. Mentored by Third Angel.

Edinburgh Fringe Festival 2017 run was supported by Underbelly (through the Underbelly Untapped Award).

CHARACTERS

ALICIA, 25

The performer playing Alicia multi-roles.

*

MUM, DAD and GREAT GREAT GRANDFATHER's
voiceovers are spoken in Yoruba and subtitled
into English for the audience.

CHARACTERS

PREFACE FROM YOLANDA MERCY

A play about family

A play about dad

A play about weddings

A play about learning not to rely on mum so much

A play about leaving Neverland

A play about hope

A play about play

A play about growing up

16-25 year old railcards

Today is the last day with my 16-25 railcard, but I'm not ready to give it up. Ready to grow up. Ready to leave the *young adult world* and become an **adult**. When I arrive at my ninth zero hour contract, part-time job ready to quit – I realise that my time for quitting may be over, and I may have to face the facts of growing up, knowing that I'm totally under-prepared.

PRE SHOW

The show begins as soon as the audience walk through the door. Even the Front of House team are part of this experience, wearing plain white T-shirts with 'Quarter Life Crisis' written in clean bold black font.

The atmosphere is upbeat and very interactive, as if you have just stepped into a party organised by Skepta and Drake. Within the space there are a series of things for the audience to interact with, buy or do. This should range from (but not be limited to):

- An Instagram style picture frame with #QuarterLifeCrisis written on the bottom for audience members to take pictures with

- A board for audience members to write a response to 'An adult is......'

- Beer pong

- A stand to buy 'Quarter Life Crisis' T-shirts, badges, play texts

There should be a screen projecting ALICIA's life story/journey as a series of GIFs. These GIFs compliment the upbeat, vibrant, millennial world that ALICIA lives in. They should start with 'QUARTER LIFE CRISIS' and should include the #QuarterLifeCrisis. The following could be used as potential plotlines for the GIF stories:

Who is Alicia Adewale?
Where is she from?
Who/what are her inspirations?
Growing up in 21st century Britain

In addition to what is in the space you can also hear loud commercial hits playing, from Hip hop, AfroBeats, R&B and Grime.

As soon as the Front of House team say, 'House is now open' the GIFs should change and just the words:

QUARTER LIFE CRISIS
Alicia Adewale
#QuarterLifeCrisis

should flash on the screen.

The music continues as the audience sit down.

ALICIA enters once everyone is seated.

It is 11am, Saturday 10th June, the day of TEE TEE's wedding, and ALICIA has two hours to be there and find a date.

ALICIA is wearing her silk bed headscarf, a black velvet vest top with a green vest top underneath, and pink Pokémon pyjama bottoms. She is bare foot. Her make up is done for the wedding, but her focus is on her iPhone. She is scrolling through Tinder for a date. The guys that she is scrolling through are projected for the audience to see. ALICIA scrolls through a series of guys, swipes left, swipes right, enlarges photos, starts to type a message which is intercepted...

Beat.

ALICIA scoffs and screws up her face. Her Tinder chat is intercepted:

'Incoming call from Dad'

Beat.

She rejects the call and diverts it to voicemail. Then puts her phone away.

Pause.

ALICIA:

> Totally under-prepared
> Totally under-educated

Beat.

> well that's a lie

ALICIA's phone notification intercepts:

She looks briefly then puts her phone away.

'cause I've got eleven GSCEs
One BTEC First
BTEC National Diploma
Two A-Levels
One BA
and an MA

Beat.

More than qualified
more than capable
more than able

Beat.

But I'm totally under-prepared
under life skilled
under aware
underwear –

– Mum, where's my underwear?

Beat.

don't really know where my birth certificate is
don't have my own place
don't even know how to assemble an IKEA bed

Beat.

But who does?
Got Mum on speed dial for the somethings
the nothings
the everythings –

– Mum, should I take this job?

V/O ALICIA (AGE **8**): Mum…

ALICIA (*On stage.*): What's for dinner?

V/O ALICIA (AGE **16**): Mum…

ALICIA (*On stage.*): What does pro-rata mean?

V/O ALICIA (AGE **24**): Mum…

ALICIA (*On stage.*): How do I get home from here?

Last one's a lie…

ALICIA: Hey Siri, How do I get home from here?

V/O SIRI: Sorry I don't understand the question.

Beat.

ALICIA: Mum, how do I get home from here?

Awkward pause.

Realised that I was totally under-prepared

undercooked

under ready

at 18

Beat.

Music and lights change to symbolise the 'luxurious' life of an 18 year old student with £4,000 from student finance in their bank account and living in a council flat.

ALICIA's four housemates are projected behind her (they must be diverse and have a variety of accents), they all call out, 'MUM!'

Beat.

We were strangers
To clubbing friends
To best friends
To performing an exorcism in *her* room
To Sunday roasts
To Wetherspoons
To make ups
To break ups
To her dad who just got out of prison

'for not committing murder'

standing in *our* kitchen <u>threatening to kill us</u>

Beat.

The housemates turn their backs to the audience.

Slowly I hated her

quickly she hated him

suddenly we hated each other

Pause.

Especially when he told everyone at Uni
          that she washes with Dettol
                  'cause she's got chlamydia

Beat.

No more Sunday roasts down Wetherspoons
No more cultural exchanges about Newcastle
No more being cold
'cause they wouldn't put the heating on

Just packed bags
        unsaid goodbyes
            and my uncle's van back to mum's

Beat.

Back to being a semi-grown up
          18+ oyster card
               discounted travel
                    discounted responsibilities
                        discounted pressure

Well at least 'til I turn 26…

Beat.

Music style shifts.

The equation below is projected but also read out by ALICIA.

<u>Discounted equations</u>

Me + 5 vodka red bulls ÷ 🍾🍾🍾🍾🍾 – 3am 💀 +
waking up at 7am – 😴 for 50 minutes x begging mum to
drop me for lecture ÷ being stuck in 🚦 for 40 minutes =
lecture just on time with a hangover

She high fives an audience member.

Beat.

No stress
head down
dictator on
laptop making notes

(benefits of being dyslexic)

Teachers understand that…

25% of my class are dyslexic

10% have dyspraxia

20% anxious

45% other

She knows that we don't wanna be there
we can't be arsed to be here
So on the first day of our first year we laid out the terms of
our unwritten contracts:

*'We students of this fine institute understand that
we are paying £9,250 a year (£16,740 if you're
international), to learn, master and perfect our
knowledge. However, there may be points where
this is compromised due to lack of sleep, excessive
drinking and passing out on MDMA. But we do
promise to try and turn up on time, sleep silently
and let our laptops or dictators do the work.'*

We kept that promise

held our bond

stayed true to our word

in return we were honoured with 2:1s

Ready for the world
Ready for anything
Ready to confront the fact that I was the *only* black person
in my year

A year of 80 students

80 students in **London**

80 students in **<u>Deptford</u>**

Beat.

Have you been to Deptford?

An image of Deptford is projected.

Well the Deptford I used to know

The modern image of Deptford is scratched out and an image of Deptford circa 2013 is projected.

Beat.

The place where I left my debt
      stripped of the title
         the student title
            and drop kicked into the real world

Slight music shift.

Beat.

By the time she was **21** my mum had had me

By the time he was **23** my grandad had travelled the world opening churches

By the time he was **24** my great, great grandfather was a slave working on a plantation

Extended pause.

As the voiceover of ALICIA's great, great grandfather reads the poem below aloud in Yoruba, vivid and thought-provoking images from British-Nigerian history (1850-2017), i.e. slavery, Fela Kuti, 'No Irish, no Blacks, no Dogs', Skepta winning the Mercury Prize etc., and English subtitles are projected.

During this ALICIA gets changed into her 'wedding outfit' – a fitted Dashiki top. She takes off her headscarf, fixes her hair and puts on black Nike Roshe Ones.

V/O GREAT, GREAT GRANDFATHER:

They put a cross on my lips, now I'm scratching at their grips
searching for a way to leave my mark
Ingrained in me to never be
that person who steps out of line
I swerve, curve and leave my clues on the fields

    Rebelliously
          Ambitiously

Hoping that someone understands
as he cracks a whip on our futile mind
I push all the notions of his limitations away
They squeeze the ink from my wrists
so I stitch up my wounds with the thoughts of you
Thoughts of him
    Thoughts of her
          Thoughts of us
thoughts of where you can be free
free from the bonds that lock me to this place

Space

Where my screams haunt our heavenly Father
who's turned his back on us
who's forsaken us
patiently
I ambivalently
Wait for him to hear

The projections fade out.

Beat.

We go back to ALICIA in present day London.

ALICIA:

I come from a line of warriors
strong fighters
Who aren't afraid to stand up for what they believe
My present warrior is my mother
who sticks her middle finger up to a system she knows won't
        accept
            acknowledge
                understand her

She stands strong
Firm
Like those who came before her
Like those who will come after her
Those she will resemble
those she has mothered

Beat.

She always wanted something to love
so she had me
someone that would unconditionally appreciate her
Grow with her
Think with her
Look after her
but she never really thought about him.
'Him' who would own a part of that unconditional love
'Him' who was still trying to find his inner warrior
so he left
turned away
only six months into my chapter
so I waited
Waited at school
Bus stops
Outside our home
Line after paragraph

paragraph after page
page after chapter
chapter after book
New book
New chapter
New century
Quarter century
of waiting
Waiting for him

Beat.

Why did you leave?
Was it something I did or said?
or should have said?
'Cause I loved you both the same –
– love you both the same
Even if I don't show it

Beat.

Showing love hasn't always been my strong point
we don't usually do that
don't usually express it
we show love in other ways like
'Have you washed out the bath?'
'Did you finish the Jollof?'
'Why are you lying? Tell the truth and shame the devil'

Beat.

Found out that this form of love was unique to my tribe
instead of words of truth
lists of complaints
Some people are greeted with the vilest invasion of personal
space –

Beat.

– **<u>Hugs</u>**

The most disgusting thing I've experienced in my whole life but *so* addictive.

Mastering the art of a good hug is kinda like a special skill.

ALICIA beckons someone from the audience to hug and does some light improvisation i.e 'Ahh yes I can see you're a hugging pro' etc. The third (last) person that she picks becomes her date for the wedding.

What's your name?…

She waits for their response.

Tinder 'It's a Match!' appears on the projection.

…I walk in late with (*insert audience members name*)
who I met like 30 seconds ago
Thanks to Tinder
He thinks something might happen after this
but I just needed a plus one for my cousin's wedding
Knew I couldn't roll up late without a date
couldn't bare the shame
Didn't want aunties setting me up with their freshie friends

Beat.

We confidently enter the wedding
sit together and act like we've know each other for time

ALICIA improvises with her 'Tinder date' but is intercepted by a phone notification:

The chat is intercepted by an incoming call from her DAD. She sees the call then puts her phone back into her pocket and smiles at her 'Tinder date'.

Sorry about that

Beat.

Perfect strangers to perfect silence
Wedding to reception
Deception to victory
'Til the heavily pregnant bride comes over
ready for war
ready to call me out on my bullshit
she studies me
then him
turns up her lip and says

TENIKA: Who's dis?

ALICIA: Tee Tee this is my date *(she beckons the audience member to say their name again)*

TENIKA: Okayyyy. How long 'ave you known eachuva for den?

ALICIA: Well erm… *(she beckons the audience member to help her say a time period)*

TENIKA: Okayyyy. *(Beat.)* You brought some random in flames to my weddin'. Are you mad? *(Beat.)* Sorry bruv, but you 'ave to leave.

Beat.

TENIKA gives him a wedding favour.

TENIKA: Fanks for comin though

Audience member sits down.

TENIKA: Cus. Wat's the matta wiv you? Don't you eva grow up? Doin' dat shit was cool when we were younger, but now we 'ave to upgrade ourselves

ALICIA: Tee Tee –

TENIKA: – it's not Tee Tee no more. It's Tenika. I'm married now. I'm not some gash on road. I've found da one 'n' you shud too cus. (*Beat.*) Stop fuckin' about online 'n' wearin' shit like dis… You're gonna be like 26 in like a week. Find yourself a nice man 'n' settle down like me. 'Cause I used to be a hoe.

ALICIA: But I'm not a hoe –

TENIKA: – yea…alrite. I'm just sayin' though cus. I used to be a hoe. (*Beat.*) But now I've reformed. I've found da one dat I wanna be with for the rest of my life…and you can too…

The wedding DJ plays 'Once upon a time' by Mariah Lynn, which intercepts TENIKA's thought.

                              …oh my days dis is my jam

TENIKA exits.

Music slowly transitions to club music.

Beat.

Don't really like clubs
the whole heel situation ain't for me
But after Tee Tee's wedding I needed some time out with my girls
Heena, Buki and Sarah
Luckily we know this Nigerian spot that don't really care what's on your feet
as long as you spend money.
Drink after drink
Drake after D'banj
Minutes to hours
clear head to twisted reality
Me to him
our lips about to intertwine until my usual thoughts splurt out

ALICIA: Do you have herpes of the mouth?

CALUM: No

Beat.

ALICIA:

Success

He understands that I'm a bit strange

guess he is too

I'm not like your average girl

worrying about getting murdered on the first night of going
back to his

instead my fears consist of herpes of the mouth, chlamydia
of the throat slash eye, and HIV

even though I use protection all the time

But what happens to the stuff that spills over the edges?

Beat.

Thoughts to reality

Club to Morleys

1 piece chicken, 3 wings, chips and a strawberry Mirinda
best believe he paid.

Peckham to Uber

    Camberwell road to his front door

        Wedding clothes to underwear

           under aware…

(*To CALUM.*) …I ran out of knickers so I borrowed my mums

CALUM: It's cool

ALICIA: Nervous to feeling accepted
     Seconds to minutes to hours

     In his bed

         his arms

            his sweat

(*To CALUM.*) your bed is really comfortable

CALUM: Yeah I know. (*Beat.*). It's me dad's.

Beat.

ALICIA:

Feeling comfortable to strawberry Mirinda travelling up
my oesophagus
3am to 6am
In his dad's bed
>   his dad's sweat
>   his dad's sex

Fuzzy mind running over sums to get me out of this equation

The equation below is projected but also read out by ALICIA.

Me + 3 hours x waiting for him to 😴 + escaping from his
dad's bed – him waking up + me getting dressed x him asking
to meet again + me inserting the wrong digits 📱 = en route
to work via 🍔🍩 before breakfast is over

Slight music shift.

We are in ALICIA's work place Lush. She looks around for ASHLEY.

Beat.

By the time he was **22** my dad started training to be a doctor

By the time she was **23** my grandmother left Nigeria for a
better life in England

By the time she was **24** my great grandmother was
crowned queen of her tribe

Beat.

For some reason the smell of Ashley's perfume
mixed with these baths bombs is making me sick
usually the fusion of scents makes the shift go quicker
But today I just want to run away

>   **again**

this is my ninth zero hour part-time contract in like two years – I've been a:

Waitress   Librarian

                Gift Wrapper

                                    Receptionist

        Cinema Usher

                        Call Centre Advisor

Bartender

and worked in WHSmith for 3 hours...

...'cause my manager made me spend 15 minutes lining up the Mentos for a customer to ruin my hard work in like 5 seconds –

So I left

                quit

                        came here

Been loyal to here for over 2 months
even if here isn't that loyal to me.
Makes me set mousetraps
Be constantly nice
and try out their products on everyone who walks in.
Luckily I have Ashley
who like me is constantly changing jobs
fearful of commitment to a desk and stability
plus finding ways to cheat the system and keep our young persons railcard.

ASHLEY: Alicia. (*Beat.*) I'm handing in my notice today

ALICIA: What?

ASHLEY: I need to grow up. Be an adult who leaves tips at restaurants, and actually pays for a drink instead of getting

tap water. I can't do that here. They don't pay us enough.
I need stability, prospects, a career.

ALICIA: In what?

ASHLEY: I don't know. But I have to leave here to find out.

ALICIA: *(To the audience.)*

All of a sudden she looks different to me.
Like I don't even know her anymore.
We were like Pinky and The Brain
Us versus the system
then the system got her
drew her in with a pro-rata contract and paid holidays.
Benefits that allowed her to abort our plan and commit to
an adult travel card.

What's the deal with growing up...
What makes you a grown up?

ALICIA asks one member of the audience, then waits for their response.
She lightly improvises with them. Then asks SIRI:

ALICIA: Hey Siri, when will I become a grown-up?

V/O SIRI: I don't know when.

Farewell bath bombs
and bitter sweet goodbyes
Like your mum leaving you at school for the first time.

Hop on the 87 bus back to ends with my

      discounted responsibilities

        discounted pressure

          discounted emotions

Battle 18 flights of stairs
'cause the lift is broken again
unbolt the door and the familiar smells of Lagos lick me in
the face.
Mum pokes her head out of the kitchen and smiles

Am I about to get a beating?
Did I forget to wash out the bath?

Beat.

Rush to my room and layer up for war
even put on a hat and ear muffs
'cause mums accuracy for landing a hit ain't always on point

ALICIA's phone notification intercepts:

ALICIA blocks CALUM on Facebook.

Beat.

The voiceover below is spoken in Yoruba but ALICIA responds in English.

V/O MUM: Oluwafemi Alicia Ife Adewale oy a wa!

ALICIA:

Shit
when Mum calls my full name I know it's about to go down.
Breeze into the living room with my armour on
position myself on the edge of the sofa ready to bolt
then Mum shouts out from the kitchen

V/O MUM: Where were you after Tee Tee's wedding?

Beat.

ALICIA:

Silence creeps over our living room
whilst I search for the perfect lies to clutter the space
I'm 25 and still bend the truth when it comes to Mum 'cause:

'There's no sex before marriage. Amen. Don't let the devil
take your life, or your womb. Or let these oyinbo people
confuse you. I bind it in Jesus name.'

Beat.

V/O MUM: Well?

ALICIA: The hairdressers

V/O MUM: Haa! And you're wearing a hat.

ALICIA:

I say nothing
        I know she knows that I'm lying
                but allows it for some reason.

Pounded Yam and Egusi Soup perfumes the air as Mum
enters the room, puts the plate in front of me and smiles

again

This time making a point

She sits down next to me with no food

and just stares

investigating my face.

Is she trying to find the perfect place to land a slap?

Beat.

Head down Pounded Yam
Egusi Soup
just keep eating

Beat.

But as the seconds turn to minutes
I can feel her eyes penetrating into my soul
She reaches her arms out and I flinch

as she draws me in close

for a hug

we never hug
is she killing me with kindness?
I try to pull away
But she draws me closer and says, 'I love you'
what the fuck!
Was she on Camberwell Road this morning?
Spotted me from the 36 bus and concocted an all-too-sweet
revenge to show me pepper
Is this how I –

V/O from MUM intercepts the thought.

V/O MUM: – your dad called me. Your grandad's dead.

Extended pause.

Lights slowly bleed out.

Silence.

We hear the sounds of birds tweeting.

Lights slowly fade up.

Over time the sounds of an animated Streatham High Street begin to underline the scene.

ALICIA is on stage in all black except for the Gele.

ALICIA:

4 days after Tee Tee's wedding
Pounded Yam to awkward silence
prayer after prayer
Stockwell to funeral
2 hours
1 train strike
numerous phone calls

          no uber

              no lift

bus replacement service
Streatham High Street
headphones in
3 stops
Ticket inspector's giving me aggro
'cause my oyster card didn't tap properly
£60 fine

      tears

        frustration

as I walk in late to my grandad's funeral.
Luckily we're Nigerian so nothing starts on time
sit in the back as I try to hide my shame
the one time I decide not to rely on Mum this happens.
Cousins walk in late after me and beckon me over to the front
To join their tribe

        his tribe

         Dad's tribe

Never felt like I was one of them
Always an outsider looking in
A part-timer in a family whose history weaved so deep that
my string didn't belong in their pattern
Cut from a different cloth
even though we look the same but have different surnames
different entry points
through him
who married her
so is the cousin to them
and is the uncle of mine
brother to Dad
Father to them all
Grandfather to us all.

Beat.

Dad leans forward, looks at me
and coats his tears with a wave
I wave back then sink deep into my seat
as the beat of the first hymn begins.
Speech after psalm
Prayer after mud
Our tribe carefully planting the seed of our founder into
the ground.
Then interlocking our fingers to unify for the first time in
my existence.
From grave side to church hall
and countless people expressing their condolences for our loss.
But as the day turns to night, our grief turns into a celebration
of life
Honouring him who travelled the world opening churches
saving lives, saving us.
We're guided down memory lane by elders who show us
dances learnt from those who came before them.
Weaving together our history of movement from Ivory Coast,
Benin, Nigeria, France then England

4th generation

3rd generation

2nd generation

1st

of people to call this place home

but so aware of where we've come from.

Elders take pleasure in reminding us that our names are clues to the journey that we've made

The meaning of ALICIA's name is projected on the screen behind:

Oluwafemi	God loves me
Alicia	Noble one
Ife	Love
Adewale	Crown has come

Beat.

Dad walks over to say hi

but before we can unlock our vaults

elders grab him by the arm to give him a history lesson.

Stuffed with knowledge that links me back to the crowning

I leave the celebration

hop on the 59 bus to ends

Weighed down with tupperware overflowing with food to stimulate my enlightened mind.

Music shift.

The equation below is projected but also read out by ALICIA.

Me – 1 day x appealing the 🚌 fine + a day off work ÷ inviting Dad to my 🎂 party on Sunday = en route to Tee Tee's 🚿 shower via TK Maxx to get a 🎁

Beat.

3pm it starts
      Proud
          Traditional
Late.

As Tee Tee's one bed flat becomes the ultimate day and night rave.

We act conservative as our mums gently usher aunties and elders around.
The echoes of Bawo ni
and kneeling becomes a strong symbol in this Engl-erian flat
as us English – Nigerians honour old traditions within our western existence.
Church songs
Local gossip
and countless hours spent praying over Tee Tee
leading us into 9pm.
Well past their bedtime
allowing us children to stay up and party.
The sounds of gospel morphs into the rhythm and bassline of grime
As Skepta leaks out of the window and down the estate walls.
From Nigerian traditions to traditions from the ends
drinking
music
heated debates like:

ALICIA asks the audience.

If you had a daughter what would you teach her?

What age do you give her a phone?

When do you tell her about sex?

From question to answer

To phone a friend

or ask the audience

Our conversation starts to unravel into something deeper

'til Tee Tee intercepts with a public service announcement

TENIKA:

Okayyy. Okayy. Bringin' it back to me, yeah. Fanks for comin'…just to clear a few fings up…'cause I know a couple girls in dis room love to chat yeah. (*Beat.*) I know you lots fought I was pregnant before, 'cause of dat one time my period was bare late after dat dickhead gave me an STI… (*Beat.*) Anyway. Dis time STI free. I'm having a baby. Marvin and I are bare excited…'cause we're the first in our families to 'ave grandkids. So hopefully you lots weren't tight, and got us bangin' gifts…'cause best believe I will name and shame. (*Beat.*) So if your gift ain't up to scratch yeah, just contribute towards the push gift…and for those of you who don't know what a push gift is essentially I get a present for pushin' the baby out of my pum pum. (*Beat.*) Marvin is buyin' me a Louis Vuitton bag. (*Beat.*) So in like three minutes he's gonna walk around wiv da card machine – we accept Visa debit, Amex, Apple pay anything really…so don't be tight 'cause the Lord sees your heart and I see your wallet. You get me.

You know that moment when you don't know what to say, so you say nothing.

That was the general consensus as Marvin patrolled the room with the card machine.

Even I contributed a percentage of my salary to the cause.

Beat.

Once adequate deposits were made

the party resumed

drink after drink

Stormzy into The Weeknd

Waking up on Saturday morning curled up on Tee Tee's sofa
with her next to me like old times.
Reminding me of the days when we used to wake up at
3pm, hit Nando's then go back to raving.
The days when our only worries consisted of
Box braids or Brazilian hair
Air force ones or 6-inch heels
stay on ends or travel to the West End
Now all I seem to think about is what am I doing with my life?
She's married, got a flat and having a baby
even Ashley's settled into a regular pattern…
But me
I feel like I'm floating
trying to escape commitment
stay in Neverland
A place where I swipe left
swipe right to find the perfect match
job
partner

Discounted responsibilities
          discounted problems
                    discounted travel

Constantly trying to perform miracles like Jesus and turn
tap water into bottomless soda at Nando's.
Mum says Rome wasn't built in a day.
But every time I scroll through my timeline I'm bombarded
with people who seem to know where they're going
what they're doing.
Do you have to know where you're going in life?
Or is it ok to make it up as you go along?

Beat.

Saturday morning to evening
still connected with her on the sofa
Studying Cookie trying to rebuild her Empire.
End of season finale to shoes on and regular goodbyes

with a slight difference.

ALICIA: Tenika, I love you

TENIKA: Luv you too cus

ALICIA:

Brixton road to outside my block a few hours before my big day

Beat.

It is 8.45am and it's ALICIA's birthday. The familiar sound of birds tweeting, neighbours playing music and Stockwell coming to life slowly underlay the scene.

By the time I was **21** I had graduated from university ready for the world even if the world wasn't ready for me

By the time I was **25** I had had nine zero hour part-time contracts desperately trying to find my perfect match

Now that I'm **26**...

Beat.

I'm late

I'm always fucking late

late crew can I get an amen?

She waits for a response.

nothing new here
except today
this morning
this hour
this minute
this second

things feel different
like they're about to change
the sun is actually shining in London
it's never sunny
except for when it's not meant to be.

The light brightens as if sunrays are streaming through blinds.

Pause.

These rays of hope
rays of joy
rays of light
make me feel like a new person
head to Vauxhall station ready to top up

iPhone message notification intercepts. ALICIA reads the reminder:

REMINDERS

Renew young persons railcard TODAY

Who decided that at 26 you should have your shit together?
Know where you're going
what you're doing
have enough money to support yourself

Why is it called a young persons railcard?
'cause if your average person lives 'til like 90, and 25 is 65
years away from that, then basically I'm a baby.
The lady behind the counter stares at me blankly

CASHIER: So do you want to renew it or not?

ALICIA:

Na don't need to
'cause I'm a…
well I think I'm a…

Beat.

ALICIA: Hey Siri, am I a grown up?

V/O SIRI: I'd rather not say.

ALICIA:

Still got Mum and Siri on speed dial for the somethings

the nothings

the everythings

still got discounted travel
Sadiq Khan's hopper
2 buses for the price of 1

Beat.

Sit on the 36 bus
down Camberwell Road
and the world feels different
I feel different
no more scamming the system
I'm legit
might even leave a tip at a restaurant

Beat.

Music shift.

I walk into my party
My 26th birthday party
late as usual
Give a nod to Tee Tee
high five to Ashley
head to the dance floor
Ready
ready for anything
ready for...

The section below is spoken in Yoruba and subtitled into English for the audience.

Dad…
Why did you leave?
Was it something I did or I said?
'cause I loved you both the same

DAD: I know you did. Do. But I wasn't ready. Able. To accept
all of the love that you had to offer, because he never
taught me. Showed me that something so precious could
love me unconditionally. Seconds after minutes. Minutes
after hours I KNOW you waited. Because I waited too.
I was there outside of your school and at the bus stop. I
saw those tears roll down your face, but I didn't know
how to mend your broken heart. Whilst I watched from
afar as your mother picked up the pieces and repaired
you. Rebuilt your strength. I was always there, but I was
too afraid to claim my place in your life because I felt like
I didn't deserve it. Deserve you. I wasn't ready to be the
father that you deserved. But now I am. If you'll let me?

Pause.

The rest of the scene continues in English.

ALICIA:

For the first time
I actually don't know what to say
but I instinctively unload my best weapon

ALICIA reaches out her arms and hugs her father (audience member).

We unwrap years of guilt
                    Anger
                         Regret

Father and daughter
stand and stare at each other
for a moment before it becomes too awkward
but long enough to know that he's here to stay.

Beat.

Mum walks over
Is there about to be a fight?
but before I can say anything she presents a peace offering
'oy ya come get Jollof'
Dad goes off with slight hesitation and joins her
united?!

Music shift.

Separated but connected
'cause of me
For this
For us
For the first time in years they stand side by side
and even smile at each other
2 similar tribes
1 common dominator
together
side by side
We may move away from each other
sway in unison together
sometimes on beat.
    off beat.
but no matter what
we stand together
Strong
like those who came before us
those who will come after us
like those we've just met
or those we just can't forget
those who don't understand us
but find a way to accept us
This is us
our tribe
our song
our movement
our voice
our history
who knows what tomorrow will bring

or replace
or displace
in this place
amidst the crisis
my quarter life crisis
I feel ready for the next chapter

Beat.

I think

iPhone notification, ALICIA looks at her phone:

'Congratulations! You have a new match!'

This is intercepted by a message notification:

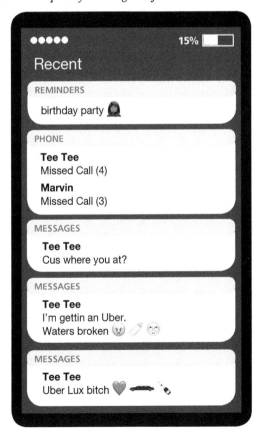

ALICIA runs off shouting.

Mum

Lights out.

Beat.

#QuarterLifeCrisis is projected.

Even though the show has ended, the party should still continue as the audience leave the theatre.

WWW.OBERONBOOKS.COM

Follow us on www.twitter.com/@oberonbooks
& www.facebook.com/OberonBooksLondon

Milton Keynes UK
Ingram Content Group UK Ltd.
UKHW020105301124
451750UK00008B/54